Charitable Planning with Charitable Trusts

By:
Mark A. Roseman, Esq.
3325 Hollywood Boulevard Suite 308
Hollywood Florida
Phone: (954) 963 - 8719; Fax: (954) 534 - 7753
www.roseman-elder-law.com

© All Rights Reserved

Mark A. Roseman

Since 1980 Attorney Mark A. Roseman has represented many clients in the field of elder law and Medicaid planning. He has frequently helped his clients preserve their assets for the stay-at-home spouse when the first spouse enters a nursing home or a living assisted facility. Attorney Roseman has drafted Charitable Trusts and prepared IRS Form 5227 form for split interest trusts since 1994.

Attorney Mark A. Roseman has participated as a student and lecturer in many seminars on issues involving Medicaid planning, asset preservation, charitable trusts and other elder law matters. As a member of the National Academy of Elder Law Attorneys, Academy of Florida Elder Law Attorneys, and Broward Estate Planning Council, he has focused primarily on these issues as they related to senior citizens. Attorney Roseman speaks without charge to planned giving and fund raising professionals.

Attorney Mark A. Roseman has delivered talks on these same issues to support groups as A.L.S. caregivers and many other organizations in South Florida. He frequently speaks under the sponsorship of the Alzheimer's Association of Greater Miami and Alzheimer's Caregiver Support, Inc. He can evaluate the suitability of equity indexed and other investments for seniors.

As a part of his Florida Elder Law and Medicaid practice Attorney Mark A. Roseman develops plans to help senior citizens and disabled individuals to qualify and maintain government benefits, including Florida Nursing Home Medicaid, Assisted Living Medicaid, Home Health Care when they have too many assets. He does estate planning and probate.

Education: Attorney Mark A. Roseman is a 1964 graduate of Dartmouth College. He graduated from Boston University Law School in 1967. Since 1980 he has practiced as a member of the Florida Bar. Due to his ethical standards and professional ability, Mark A. Roseman was awarded Martindale-Hubbell AV Preeminent Peer Review Rating.

Disclaimer

These seminar materials and the seminar presentation are intended to stimulate thought and discussion, and to provide those attending the seminar with useful ideas and guidance in the areas of estate planning and administration. The materials and the comments of Mr. Roseman do not constitute, and should not be treated as, legal advice regarding the use of any particular estate planning or other technique, device or suggestion, or any of the tax or other consequences associated with them. Although we have made every effort to ensure the accuracy of these materials and the seminar presentation, Mr. Roseman does not assume any responsibility for any individual's reliance on the written or oral information presented during the seminar. Each seminar attendee should verify independently all statements made in the materials and during the seminar presentation before applying them to a particular fact pattern, and should determine independently the tax and other consequences of using any particular device, technique or suggestion before recommending the same to a client or implementing the same on a client's or his or her own behalf.

Charitable Trusts

Outline

Introduction	4
Charitable Remainder Trusts	5
Overview, Types of CRTs	5
Duration of CRTs	7
Testing Requirements	7
Income Taxation of CRTs	8
Income Tax Charitable Deduction	8
Estate and Gift Tax Charitable Deduction	11
Planning Issues and Opportunities	13
Charitable Lead Trusts	15
Types of CLTs	15
Duration of CLTs	16
Testing and Payout Requirements of CLTs	16
Income Taxation of CLTs and the Income Tax Charitable Deduction	16
Estate and Gift Tax Charitable Deduction	17
Who Can Serve as Trustee	18
Private Foundation Restrictions	19
Charitable Planning for Smaller Gifts	19
Summary	20
Glossary	22
Sample CRT	24

INTRODUCTION

Charitable Remainder Trusts (CRTs) and Charitable Lead Trusts (CLTs) are creations of statute. They are also referred to as "split-interest" trusts. The split occurs because for a period of time the trust benefits both non-charitable and charitable beneficiaries. Their interests are successive, not joint. The significance of structuring a trust as a CRT or CLT is that it allows the Settlor/Donor to take advantage of income tax deductions and charitable estate and gift tax deductions for transfers to the trust. It is possible to create a trust that specifies "net income to individual(s) for life, remainder to charity;" however, a transfer to such a trust will not qualify for any type of charitable deduction. The structure of a CRT and CLT are similar. The difference is the timing of when the trust benefits charity. As the names indicate, a charitable lead trust is one that pays a stream of money to a charity first, with individuals receiving the remainder interest. A charitable remainder trust is one that pays a stream of money to individuals first, with the remainder interest going to charity.

A key concept for both types of trusts is that the upfront payout or lead interest (to charity in a lead trust or to individuals in a remainder trust) must be structured either as a unitrust payout or as an annuity. The duration of the lead interest can be for a fixed number of years, not exceeding twenty, or for the lifetime of one or more individuals. There is not technically a limit on the number of lives during which the lead interest is to be paid. However, charitable remainder trusts must pass actuarial tests to ensure that a certain minimum percentage of the funds actually will pass to charity.

Split-interest trusts are an excellent vehicle for the Settlor who desires to make a charitable transfer, but who either doesn't want, or can't afford, to exclude individuals from receiving any benefits from the transferred property. They also present planning opportunities using the concept of leverage. A charitable remainder trust is particularly useful as the recipient of qualified plan monies <u>at the death of the donor</u> (but not during the donor's lifetime).

CHARITABLE REMAINDER TRUSTS

Overview

There are two main types of charitable remainder trusts – charitable remainder annuity trusts (CRATs) and charitable remainder unitrusts (CRUTs). In addition, there are several different variations of CRUTs: the standard CRUT (SCRUT), the net income CRUT (NICRUT), the net income with make-up CRUT (NIMCRUT) and a flip CRUT. CRTs may be established as inter-vivos trusts or as testamentary trusts. The payout from a CRT to the non-charitable beneficiary is based upon a percentage of the fair market value of the trust assets. The minimum payout is 5% and the maximum payout is 50%. IRC 664(d)(1) and IRC 664(d)(2). With a CRAT the payout is determined at the inception of the trust, and then never changes (hence the term "annuity" trust). No matter how much the market value of the trust assets changes, the annuity payout remains constant (unless the trust declines in value to the point that it is depleted and there are no more funds to pay the annuity). Additional contributions may <u>not</u> be made to a CRAT. Reg. 1.664-2(b). If the donor desires to do another gift, he or she must create another CRAT.

In a CRUT, the trust is revalued on an annual basis, and the percentage stated in the document is applied to the (new) value every year. Reg. 1.664-3(a)(1)(1)(a). If the market value of the trust increases then the CRUT payment increases. Likewise, if the market value of the trust declines, then the CRUT payment will also decline. A CRUT, unlike a CRAT, may receive additional contributions during its term. Reg. 1.664-3(b)(1) and (2). Thus, a donor who desires to make additional gifts can simply add more property to an existing CRUT. The minimum frequency of the payout is annual for both a CRAT and a CRUT, although it can be more frequently. Quarterly payouts are common.

A NICRUT is a CRUT that states that the trustee is to pay out the lesser of the trust's net income or the stated percentage amount. IRC 664(d)(2) and (3). A NIMCRUT directs the trustee to pay out the lesser of the trust's net income or the stated percentage amount with an additional feature that the trustee is to make up deficiencies from earlier years (i.e. years when the net income was less than the stated percentage amount) in years that the net income exceeds the stated payout amount. IRC 664(d)(2) and (3). Finally, a FLIP CRT is one that will change from either a NICRUT or NIMCRUT to a SCRUT upon the occurrence of a triggering event, such as the sale of a non-marketable asset used to fund the CRT. The event cannot be something within the discretion of the trustee. Permissible events include marriage, divorce, death, and birth. The sale of non-marketable assets may also be a triggering event. Once the triggering event occurs, the flip takes place not in the year of the occurrence, but in the following year. After the flip, any make up amount from a NIMCRUT is forfeited.

In the year that either type of CRT is initially funded or the year that it terminates, it is most likely to be a short year – i.e. not a full 365 days. (It is unusual for a CRT to be funded on January 1st, and income beneficiaries don't always die on December 31st.) In both of these instances, the income payout is prorated based upon the partial year. Reg. 1.664-2(a)(1)(iv) and 1.664-3(a)(1)(v). A similar computation is done for a mid-year addition to an existing CRUT. Reg. 1.664-3(b)(1) and (2).

The trust agreement can specify which day of the year is to be used to value the trust. Most documents provide that the valuation is to be done either on the first day of each taxable year or on the first business day of each taxable year.

Duration of CRTs

A CRT (both annuity and unitrust varieties) can be set up for the income payout to last for a term of years, not exceeding 20, or for the lifetime of one or more income recipients. There is not technically a limit on the number of lives to whom the payout can be made. However, when the payout is based on someone's life that "someone" has to be alive at the time the trust is created. This leads to the question of when is a CRT created? For an inter-vivos CRT, the creation date is the date it receives funding. For a testamentary CRT, it is the date of death.

If, however, a trust is set up to pay out for a term of years, then during that term the payments can be made to a class of beneficiaries, some of whom might not be born at the time the trust is created. It is possible to have the income distributed on a "sprinkle-spray" basis among the members of the class. However, it is important that the Trustee not be the Settlor or a party subordinate to the Settlor if this provision is included.

Testing Requirements

One test that a CRAT (but not a CRUT) must pass is the 5% Probability Test. If there is more than a 5% probability that the trust assets will be exhausted prior to the end of the measuring term (i.e. prior to the charity receiving the remainder interest), then transfers to the trust will not qualify for income, gift and estate tax charitable deductions. A second test that __all__ CRTs must pass is that the present value of the charitable remainder interest of the trust must be at least 10% of the value of the trust at the time that it is funded. There are reformation rules in place in order to permit a CRT that fails the 10% test to either reduce the payout rate or the measuring term in order to qualify the trust.

Income Taxation of CRTs (Tax-Exempt Status)

One of the marvelous benefits of a CRT is that it is a tax-exempt entity at the trust level. Unless a CRT has unrelated business taxable income (UBTI), it will not pay tax at the trust level. IRC Section 664(c). However, distributions from the trust to the income recipient do carry out taxable income, based on the 4 tier system of accounting, as follows:

Tier One: Ordinary (taxable) income

Tier Two: Capital gains

Tier Three: Other income (i.e. tax-exempt income)

Tier Four: Return of principal

Note that this is a different system of income being carried out, or distributed, to beneficiaries than exists for traditional irrevocable trusts. In those trusts ordinary income (taxable and tax-exempt) is carried out proportionately and capital gains generally stay within the trust and are taxed to the trust.

CRTs frequently have a significant amount of tier two (capital gain) income within the trust. If the trustee sells an appreciated asset and reinvests the proceeds in municipal tax-exempt bonds, the capital gains will be distributed to the income recipient and the tax-exempt income remains within the trust (which is a tax-exempt entity). This can be a trap for the unknowledgeable trustee.

Even though a CRT is tax-exempt at the trust level, the trustee still needs to obtain cost basis information from the donor on the property contributed to the trust. The trustee is also required to file income tax returns (informational in nature). These include Form 5227 and IT-41. CRTs are required to be on calendar tax years. IRC Section 645.

It used to that if a CRT had any UBTI in a taxable year the consequence was that all the trust's income for that tax year was subject to income taxes – i.e. the trust lost its tax-exempt status for the that taxable year. Reg. 1.513-1(b). This has, fortunately, been changed. Instead a 100% excise tax is imposed upon UBTI in a CRT, but the trust is able to keep its tax-exempt status.

Retention of Right to Change Charitable Beneficiaries/Alternate Remainderman

It is permissible for the grantor of the CRT to retain the right in the trust agreement to change the charitable beneficiaries who will ultimately receive the property. Rev. Rul. 76-8, 1976-1 C.B. 179; PLR 2000-34-019 (May 25, 2000). The trust must also contain a provision that provides for an alternate charitable remainder beneficiary to be selected in the event the original named charity does not exist or is not qualified as a charity.

Income Tax Charitable Deduction

When a donor funds a CRT during lifetime, he or she is entitled to a charitable income tax deduction. The deduction is not, however, for the full value of the property contributed to the trust. Rather, it is for the present value of the future interest that will pass to charity at the end of the distribution period.

There are eight factors that affect the amount of the charitable income tax deduction. These are:

- The net fair market value of the property transferred
- Whether the CRT is an annuity trust or a unitrust.
- The payout factor of the CRT.

- The duration of the up-front income distribution period [term of years, lifetime(s) of income recipient(s)].

- The frequency of the payment of the income distribution (annual, semi-annual, quarterly.

- The amount of time that elapses between the valuation date and the first payment date.

- Whether the payout occurs at the beginning of the period or end of the period.

- The Applicable Federal Mid-term Rate.

As you might expect, the younger the income recipient (for duration measured by life expectancy) or the longer the term (fixed years), the lower the charitable deduction. The more income recipients (for example, in a trust using consecutive life estates as the measuring term) the lower the charitable deduction. The higher the payout amount, the lower the charitable deduction. The imposition of the 10% minimum present value of the remainder interest has the effect of disqualifying CRTs for young donors.

The calculation of the present value of the charitable remainder interest uses unisex mortality tables. The discount rate used in the calculation is 120% of the AFMR in the month of the gift. The donor may also elect to use the AFMR from one of the two months preceding the gift.

If the income recipient is terminally ill at the time of the funding of the CRT, then the standard actuarial tables and discount rules do not apply. A terminally ill person is someone who is known to have an incurable illness with a 50% probability of death within one year.

The steps in which the present value of the remainder interest is determined is actually to value the up-front income interest and then subtract that from the total amount of the transfer to the CRT. The difference is the value of the remainder interest. Although it is possible to do the calculations manually (and in the dark ages this author did so), a number of software programs are available that do the calculations. The deductibility of the charitable gift for income tax purposes is subject to the same rules as other charitable income tax deductions (percent of income tests, carry forward, etc.). IRC Section 170. Note the differences for income tax purposes of naming a 30 percent type charity versus a 50 percent type charity as remainderman. When a power of substitution is retained you want to make sure that the substituted charity is required to be of the same type as the removed charity.

Estate and Gift Tax Charitable Deduction

When a CRT is created and funded during the donor's lifetime, then he or she is entitled to a charitable gift tax deduction for the present value of the remainder interest that will eventually pass to charity. The amount of the charitable gift tax deduction is the same as the charitable income tax deduction. If there is an income recipient other than the donor, then he or she has also made a <u>taxable</u> gift. Depending upon the terms of the trust, the donor may be able to use the annual gift tax exclusion for the non-charitable portion of the gift, based on the present interest rules. For example, if the donor is the initial income recipient and the donor's child has a consecutive life interest that begins at the donor's death, the child does not have a present interest in the trust, and the annual exclusion will not available for the gift to the child. Gifts that are either in excess of the annual exclusion or that do not qualify for the annual exclusion may be offset by the donor's credit shelter amount. The donor may retain a testamentary power to revoke an income beneficiary's interest. Reg. 1.664-2(a)(4) [CRATs} and Reg. 1.664-3(a)(4) [CRUTs]. In this case, there is not a completed gift to that (potential) income recipient.

If a donor creates a lifetime CRT reserving the income interest for himself, then at death the full value of the CRT will be pulled back into the donor's estate for federal estate tax purposes. The estate tax consequences of the CRT depend on whether the trust continues for non-charitable beneficiaries or terminates in favor of the charity at the death of the donor. In the latter case, there is a wash from a tax standpoint. The full value of the trust is pulled into the estate, but then the estate can take a charitable deduction for the full value of the trust.

When an inter-vivos CRT that continues for other non-charitable beneficiaries is pulled back into the estate, then the estate goes through the process of redetermining the present value of the remainder interest. This also occurs if a CRT if funded (for the first time) at the death of the donor. In both cases, the determination is made using the mortality tables, AFMR, the duration of the non-charitable interest (term of years versus lifetime), etc.

It is particularly important that the CRT document prohibit the payment of federal estate taxes from the CRT. Rev. Rule 82-128, 1982-2 C.B. 71. One option for providing for the payment of the taxes is to include a provision that requires the income beneficiary to provide the funds for the taxes attributable to his/her interest (or else forfeit the interest). The donor may also make provisions for the federal estate taxes to be paid from other estate assets.

A CRT can be drafted in such a way as to qualify for the marital deduction. If the decedent's surviving spouse is the <u>only</u> income recipient, then the trust will qualify. IRC Section 2056(b)(8). Another option for estate planning for spouses is to create a QTIP trust under which the spouse is entitled to all the net income for life where the remainder beneficiary is a charity. The trustee can also be given the right to invade principal for the surviving spouse, which provides for more flexibility. At the death of the surviving spouse, the full value of the trust is pulled into the spouse's estate, but is entitled to an offsetting charitable deduction

Planning Issues and Opportunities

The selection of the type of CRT is important in the planning process. For example, if a standard unitrust is funded with non-income producing real estate how will the trustee make the unitrust payment? Deed out a fractional interest in the real estate? This is not a good idea for several reasons. First of all, you don't want to end up with small fractional amounts of the real estate being owned by multiple parties. If it takes a long time to sell the real estate, there will be multiple transfers out. Secondly, this can be expensive because of the need to obtain up to date valuations and legal descriptions for the pieces being carved out. Thirdly, if a CRAT or SCRUT makes an in-kind distribution, it is deemed to be a sale of the property distributed and gain will be recognized. Reg. 1.664-1(d)(6). A trust funded with non-income producing real estate is an example of when using a flip CRT makes good sense. During the time period that the CRT holds the real estate there will be no income, so the trustee will not make any distributions. The sale of the real estate can be the triggering event that will transform the NIMCRUT to a standard CRT. Because the CRT now has cash, it has the funds with which to make the unitrust distributions. Remember, however, that the beneficiary will have to wait until the following calendar year in which to receive the standard payout. You will want to remind the beneficiary of that so that he or she is not expecting a check immediately after the sale!

One of the features that makes a CRT such an important tool is the fact that it is a tax-exempt entity at the trust level. This is particularly valuable when dealing when a donor's highly appreciated assets and qualified plan assets.

It is not unusual for a donor to have assets that have appreciated significantly in value. The donor is often faced with the dilemma of selling the assets in order to create a more diversified portfolio or to generate more income, but then having to recognize capital gains on the sale. By the time the taxes are paid and the amount left after taxes is reinvested, the donor may not be getting any more income than before the sale (although he or she may have minimized some risk because of reducing a concentration). If the donor gifts the appreciated assets to the CRT, the CRT can sell them and pay no tax. The trustee then has 100% of the proceeds of the sale to reinvest and generate an income stream for the donor. The donor receives an income tax deduction for the present value of the remainder interest.

Qualified plan assets pose challenges for estate planners. Not only are the assets subject to estate tax in a decedent's estate, they retain their character as taxable income. These assets represent income in respect of a decedent (IRD). Thus, whoever inherits the qualified plan assets will still have to pay income tax on the funds – there is no step up in basis. An alternative is to use the qualified plan assets to fund a CRT at death. Because the CRT is a tax-exempt entity, it will not pay income tax on the receipt of the funds. It can invest 100% of the proceeds in order to generate the annuity or unitrust payout for the income recipient(s).

CRTs can also be useful vehicles for income deferral. For example, a donor might want to fund a CRT in a high taxable income year, thus obtaining the charitable income tax deduction. If the CRT is invested in such a way as to generate little income, then, under a NICRUT or NIMCRUT, the donor will not be receiving distributions from the trust. In later years, for example after retirement when the donor is in a lower income tax bracket, the investment strategy for the trust can be changed in order to generate income for the payout. In the meantime, the trust will have had the benefit of tax-deferred investing.

Selection of the appropriate type of CRT and appropriate and realistic payout rate are important in the planning process. For the donor who needs an assured income stream, the CRAT may be a more suitable vehicle than a CRUT. Over a long period of time in a CRUT, a lower payout <u>rate</u> may ultimately result in higher payouts during the term of the trust, due to the benefit of keeping more dollars in the trust and allowing them to grow.

From a planning standpoint, a lower interest rate environment favors charitable lead trusts, whereas higher interest rates generate higher charitable deductions for charitable remainder trusts. In the 1990s the 7520 rate ranged from 5.4% to 10.6%. In the 2000's it ranged from 2% to 8%, and since 2010 the highest it has been is 3.4%. The July 2016 rate was 1.8% and the August and September rates were 1.4%.

CHARITABLE LEAD TRUSTS

A charitable lead trust is often thought of as the reverse of a charitable remainder trust. And, to the extent that the timing of the distribution to charity is flip-flopped, this is true. However, there is a distinct set of tax rules that are very different than those that apply to charitable remainder trusts. A common theme, however, is the use of actuarial tables and the applicable federal midterm rate to determine the present value of the amount going to charity.

Types of CLTs

A charitable lead trust must be structured either as a charitable lead annuity trust ("CLAT") or a charitable lead unitrust ("CLUT. This is similar to the requirement for the income payment to the non-charitable beneficiary of a CRT to be either an annuity or unitrust amount. Additional contributions to a charitable lead annuity trust ("CLAT") cannot be made. However, additions may be made to a charitable lead unitrust ("CLUT"). The trustee may also be given the discretion to pay out trust income that exceeds the annuity/unitrust amount to the charitable beneficiary. In essence this would be paying out the <u>greater</u> of trust income or the stated annuity/unitrust amount.

Duration of CLTs

A charitable lead trust may be structured to last for a term of years or for the life of one or more individuals, each of whom must be living on the date the trust is funded. Unlike a CRT, there is no maximum term of years for which the CLT may be established, although a state's rule against perpetuities will apply.

Testing and Payout Requirements

Unlike a CRT, there are no minimums or maximums that apply to the payout rate of a CLT. In addition, neither the 5% probability test nor the 10% minimum charitable interest test applies. The payout to the charitable beneficiary or beneficiaries must be made at least annually. A charitable lead trust may have more than one charitable beneficiary, and the trustee may have the discretion to sprinkle the annuity or unitrust amount among the beneficiaries. In addition, the trustee (so long as it is not the donor) may have the right to choose a charitable recipient. (A donor may serve as the trustee, but the right to designate the recipients will cause estate tax inclusion.)

Income Taxation of CLTs and the Income Tax Charitable Deduction

A very significant difference between a CLT and a CRT is that a CLT is not a tax-exempt entity for income tax purposes. A CLT will either be taxed as a grantor trust for income tax purposes (i.e. all items of gross income and deductions will be reflected on the grantor's personal tax return) or as a complex trust. This is a choice made by how the trust instrument is drafted. It is not as simple as stating this is going to be a grantor CLT or this is going to be a complex trust CLT. In order to be a grantor trust, the trust agreement must contain provisions that would cause it to be a grantor trust under Sections 671 – 679 of the Internal Revenue Code. Care must be taken to ensure that the trust is only a grantor trust for income tax purposes without causing inclusion in the donor's estate for federal estate tax purposes.

If the CLT is created as a grantor CLT, then in the year that it is funded, the grantor may take an income tax deduction for the present value of the income stream going to charity. This is a one-time charitable income tax deduction. In the future years of the trust, all the income will be taxed to the grantor, but he or she will not receive any additional deductions. If the trust is structured as a complex trust, then the donor does not receive any income tax deduction for creating the trust. The trust will be taxed as a complex trust, but will be able to take a deduction for the amounts paid to charity. Any income earned by the trust over and above what is distributed to charity will be taxed to the trust at the high trust rates. The concept of four-tier accounting that applies to CRTs is not applicable to CLTs. Instead, the regular fiduciary income tax rules apply.

Estate and Gift Tax Charitable Deduction

As we saw in the discussion on the estate and gift tax charitable deduction for charitable remainder trusts, a calculation is done to determine the present value of the income stream that is going to go to charity in a charitable lead trust. The factors that are used in doing CRT calculations are used in CLT calculations, namely the applicable federal mid-term rate, the duration of the charitable lead period, the rate of the payout, the frequency of the payout, whether the trust is an annuity trust or a unitrust, for example.

One key difference is that there is no availability of the annual exclusion to be applied to the portion of the trust that will ultimately pass to the non-charitable beneficiary. This is because the annual exclusion is only available for gifts of a present interest. If the lead trust is one that reverts to the donor upon the expiration of the charitable lead interest, then there is no taxable gift to someone else. If, however, upon the expiration of the lead interest, the trust assets pass to other individuals, then that is a taxable gift. The donor's gift or estate tax exemption amount can be used against that portion of the gift.

WHO CAN SERVE AS TRUSTEE?

The grantor of a CRT is permitted to serve as the trustee. Care must be taken in the drafting, however, to avoid retention of powers that cause the trust to be considered a "grantor" trust, because the trust then no longer qualifies as a CRT. Such powers include the right to sprinkle spray the distribution among a class of income beneficiaries. If this feature is desired, then the grantor should not only not serve as trustee, but should be prevented from serving in the future (in other words, also review the powers to remove the trustee and appoint a successor).

Another area which can cause problems if the grantor is also serving as trustee has to do with the valuation of hard to value assets. A CRT's unmarketable assets must be appraised either by an independent trustee or by a qualified appraiser. Reg. 1.664-1(a)(7).

Important considerations in selecting the CRT trustee are costs and experience. Does the proposed trustee under the 4 tier accounting system? If a donor insists on naming a charity as the trustee, the charity may want to consider outsourcing the administration and investment of the CRT.

The considerations for a choice of trustee for a CLT are the same as for a CRT. The donor may serve, depending upon how the trust is drafted. For example, if the intent is to allow the trustee the right to select a charitable recipient, then someone other than the donor should serve as trustee and the donor should be prevented from serving in the future (in other words, also review the powers to remove the trustee and appoint a successor).

Selection of a trustee for any type of trust, whether it is a charitable split-interest trust or credit shelter trust or other type of trust should take into consideration the competence of the trustee, the time available to serve as trustee, the trustworthiness of the trustee, and costs. When evaluating costs and doing a comparison between a professional fiduciary such as a bank or trust company and an individual, remember that the individual will likely need to hire investment managers and tax professionals.

PRIVATE FOUNDATION RESTRICTIONS

CRTs and CLTs are subject to private foundation restrictions against self-dealing. Reg. 1.664-1(b). Self-dealing includes the sale, exchange or leasing of property between the CRT and a disqualified person, as well as lending money from the trust to a disqualified person. A disqualified person in relation to a CRT/CLT includes the creator of the trust, the trustee, a spouse, ancestor, child, grandchild, great grandchild and their spouses. The penalty for an act of self-dealing starts with an initial tax of 5% of the amount involved and is imposed on the disqualified person. If an act of self-dealing is not corrected, an additional tax of 200% is imposed on the disqualified person.

Other aspects of the private foundation rules that apply to split-interest trusts include rules regarding excess business holdings and jeopardizing investments.

CHARITABLE PLANNING FOR SMALLER GIFTS

One of the advantages of charitable remainder and charitable lead trusts is the ability to structure a gift in such a way as to provide monetary benefits to an individual as well as charity. A factor in establishing these trusts, however, is the cost. First of all there is the cost to have the trust drafted. Secondly, there are trustee fees to be considered, along with investment management fees and accounting fees if a professional fiduciary is not used. Professional fiduciaries usually have minimum fees that apply, that can make it cost prohibitive to use a professional trustee.

For lifetime planning, one option for the smaller gift is to fund a charitable gift annuity. This allows the donor to make a current gift, keep for himself/herself an income stream, and receive a gift tax deduction for the present value of the amount that will eventually go to charity. The donor may also have the income payout be made to a third person, instead of retaining it for himself or herself. The contract to create a charitable gift annuity is one or two pages long, typically, and is something that the charity has on hand. Not all charities offer charitable gift annuities, but it can provide an alternative for the donor with fewer assets. From an estate planning standpoint, charities are happy to receive outright bequests, even small ones.

SUMMARY

Split-interest gifts are an important part of the estate planner's toolkit. They offer clients a number of options in structuring their estates to take advantage of the tax-exempt aspects of CRTs, of leveraging the credit equivalent, and for obtaining charitable deductions for trusts that have both charitable and non-charitable beneficiaries. Great care must be taken, however, in making sure the trusts comply with the IRS Code and Regulations.

Planners who are interested in using CRTs and CLTs to help their clients accomplish their estate planning and financial goals can avail themselves of a number of low cost or free resources. These include the Central Florida Community Foundation (CICF) and its Planned Giving Design Center, which can be found at www.pgdc.com. In addition, the Partnership for

Philanthropic Planning (formerly known as the National Committee on Planned Giving) is headquartered in Florida.

In 2003 IRS issued eight new sample charitable remainder annuity trusts, which can be found in Rev. Proc. 2003-54. In 2005 IRS issued eight new charitable remainder unitrust sample documents, which can be found in Rev. Proc. 2005-52 through Rev. Proc. 2005-59. They provide a beginning point.

GLOSSARY

AFMR	Applicable Federal Mid-term Rate
CLT	Charitable Lead Trust
CLAT	Charitable Lead Annuity Trust
CLUT	Charitable Lead Unitrust
CRT	Charitable Remainder Trust
CRAT	Charitable Remainder Annuity Trust
CRUT	Charitable Remainder Unitrust
FLIP CRT	Either a NICRUT or NIMCRUT that flips to a Standard CRUT upon occurrence of a triggering event or date
NICRUT	Net Income Charitable Remainder Unitrust
NIMCRUT	Net Income with Make Up Charitable Remainder Unitrust
SCRUT	Standard Charitable Remainder Unitrust
UBTI	Unrelated Business Taxable Income

Other Terms and Definitions

Four Tier Accounting — A classification ordering system for CRTs that determines the nature of distributions <u>from</u> the CRT to the income recipient. Distributions are made first from ordinary taxable income, second from capital gains, third from tax-exempt income, and fourth from principal.

Income Recipient — The beneficiary who receives the annuity amount or unitrust amount from the CRT (to be distinguished from the income beneficiary of a "traditional" trust, who receives "net income").

Independent Trustee — A person who is not the grantor of the trust, a noncharitable beneficiary, or a related or subordinate party to the grantor, the grantor's spouse, or a noncharitable beneficiary (within the meaning of section 672©. 1.664-1(a)(7)(iii)

Qualified Appraisal — An appraisal that is prepared by qualified appraiser not earlier than 60 days prior to the date of the contribution of the property and not later than the due date of the return (and extensions), does not involve a prohibited appraisal fee and includes certain specified information. Reg. 1.170A-13(c)(3).

Qualified Appraiser — An individual who holds himself out to the public as an appraiser of the type of property being valued, is not an excluded individual and who understands the penalties for aiding and abetting an understatement of tax liability. Reg. 1.170A-13(c)(5).

Unmarketable Assets — Assets that are not cash, cash equivalents, or other assets that can be readily sold or exchanged for cash or cash equivalents. Unmarketable assets include real property, closely held stock, and an unregistered security for which there is no available exemption permitting public sale. 1.664-1(a)(7)(ii)

Mark A. Roseman, Esq.
3325 Hollywood Boulevard Suite 308
Hollywood Florida
Phone: (954) 963 - 8719; Fax: (954) 534 - 7753
www.roseman-elder-law.com

© All Rights Reserved

www.ingramcontent.com/pod-product-compliance
Lightning Source LLC
Chambersburg PA
CBHW080232180526
45158CB00010BA/3163